HOW TO BE AN
ANCIENT GREEK
ATHLETE

Written by
Jacqueline Morley

Illustrated by
David Antram

BOOK　HOUSE

Jacqueline Morley studied English at Oxford University. She has taught English and History and has a special interest in the history of everyday life. She has written historical fiction and non-fiction for children and is the author of the prize-winning **An Egyptian Pyramid** in the *Inside Story* series.

David Antram was born in Brighton, England, in 1958. He studied at Eastbourne College of Art and then worked in advertising for fifteen years before becoming a full-time artist. He has illustrated many children's non-fiction books.

Series created and designed by **David Salariya**
Editors **Michael Ford, Claire Andrews**
Fact Consultant **Dr Stephen Instone, Department of Greek and Latin, University College London**

Published in Great Britain in 2005 by
Book House, an imprint of
The Salariya Book Company Ltd
25 Marlborough Place, Brighton BN1 1UB

Please visit the Salariya Book Company at:
www.salariya.com

ISBN 1-905087-05-5
A catalogue record for this book is available from the British Library.
The Salariya Book Company operates an environmentally friendly policy wherever possible.
Printed and bound in China.

Visit our website at **www.book-house.co.uk**
for free electronic versions of:
You wouldn't want to be an Egyptian Mummy!
You wouldn't want to be a Roman Gladiator!
Avoid joining Shackleton's Polar Expedition!
Avoid sailing on a 19th-century Whaling Ship!

Photographic credits
t=top b=bottom c=centre l=left r=right

Ancient Art & Architecture Collection: 15
The Art Archive / Goulandris Foundation Athens / Dagli Orti: 23
The Art Archive / Museo Nazionale Terme Rome / Dagli Orti: 13
The Art Archive / Kanellopoulos Museum Athens / Dagli Orti: 29
The Art Archive / Archaeological Museum Delphi / Dagli Orti: 18
Shefton Museum, University of Newcastle-upon-Tyne: 11b
© Copyright The Trustees of The British Museum: 20

Every effort has been made to trace copyright holders. The Salariya Book Company apologizes for any unintentional omissions and would be pleased, in such cases, to add an acknowledgment in future editions.

Athlete Required

Good at games? Keen to compete? Got what it takes to be a winner?

If that sounds like you, the city state of Athens would like to hear from you. It is looking for strong active young people to train in a variety of sports, with a view to competing in the city's famous Panathenaic Games.

Applicants must be:

- Of freeborn parentage – slaves cannot apply.

- Obedient to their trainers in all matters, and to the rules of their chosen sport (fouls are punishable by instant whipping).

- Aware that Ancient Greek sports festivals are sacred events and one reason for competing is to honour the gods.

Job prospects are excellent. If you do well in the Athenian Games you could be chosen to represent Athens at the Great Games at Olympia and win an Olympic crown.

Apply in person at your local gymnasion.

Contents

What applicants should know

B e prepared for a long-haul timeflight to around 450 BC, your destination – Ancient Greece. This is not one country like modern Greece, but is made up of many small states, each centred on a city or town, all fiercely independent and often at war with each other. Each state needs tough menfolk to defend it. That is why athletics is so important. Almost every city has its own Games, held in honour of its protector god, and training for them keeps young people fit. The Games at Athens, the most powerful city, are a very big affair. Winning there is a step on the way to the biggest win of all – a victory at Olympia, the top athletic venue in Greece.

These Games are open to men and boys only. There are festivals for women athletes as well, although they attract much less attention, so girls, please apply too.

Ancient Greece
c.450 BC

THRACE

Area in red shows the Greek world

AEGEAN SEA

Delphi

GREECE

Athens

ASIA MINOR

Olympia

Greek islands

Sparta

MEDITERRANEAN SEA

CRETE

At the gymnasion

T his is a job opportunity in one of history's prime spots. Athens in the 5th century BC is buzzing with new ideas; its arts will inspire people for thousands of years and it has just invented democracy. You'll be training at a gymnasion, which is like a school, a university and a sports centre all in one. Boys come for lessons and games; grown men come to train or watch the practice, and to argue about life and truth.

There are recitation, music and singing contests at the Games. Older pupils also study philosophy and do archery and infantry drill.

A music lesson at the gymnasion

▼ You'll start training in a place called a *palaistra*, where you have lessons as well as games. Athenians think the mind needs to be fed and strengthened, just like the body.

What do we mean by democracy?

Philosophy

▲ In the colonnade you'll find people listening to talkers known as 'philosophers'. These are thinkers of a new, particularly Athenian kind. They're seeking answers to life's big questions – the nature of the universe; the best way for people to be governed; the right way to live a good life.

6

▼ A lecture in one of the palaistra's study rooms. All rooms open onto a colonnade that surrounds a large central courtyard, used for boxing and wrestling. There are rooms for undressing (male athletes perform naked), for washing and for storing equipment.

A teacher reciting poetry

A pupil doing a test

That everyone can vote – except women and slaves of course!

▲ This young man, about to become a citizen, is taking a compulsary two-year course on the city's traditions.

Greek literature

▶ You'll hear poetry and drama that's among the world's all-time best.

A fragment by the great female poet, Sappho

Girls' education

◀ Girls and boys don't train together. That's frowned on in Athens, though it's normal in the state of Sparta. That's why disapproving Athenians call Spartan girls 'thigh flashers'. In Athens girls study at home, learning womanly skills, and train at women's palaistras, often attached to a temple of Artemis, goddess of hunting.

Sport and recreation

The Greeks believe in bettering their bodies as well as their minds, and place a great deal of importance on physical exercise. As well as athletics at school, young boys like you play a number of games outside the gymnasion. So remember, although they are only games, they will help sharpen your competitive edge and keep you fit.

Ball skills

▼A boy balances a ball made from a pig's bladder on his thigh while holding his hands behind his back. He keeps the ball in the air by bouncing it back and forth from one knee to the other.

Hockey

▶A fast and furious type of hockey was played in pairs. Players 'face off' and, using a curved stick, aim to push the ball or disc over their opponents' line.

That's it. You're over the back line!

Team games

▲Boys play *episkyros*, a game played by two teams of equal numbers. A line is drawn between them and another behind each team. A ball is placed on the central line. Each team tries to throw the ball past the other, who must try to stop it and throw it back again. The winning team is the one that manages to throw the ball past the opposition, driving them over their back line.

▲ Another favourite Greek team game is called *ephedrismos* in which a *dioros* (stone) is set up at a distance and two players compete to knock it over by throwing balls. The loser has to give the other a piggy-back and then try to find the dioros, with his 'rider' covering his eyes!

OK. You win!

Acrobatics

▶ Acrobatics are popular. Acrobats are used as children's entertainers. In this acrobatic stunt a man vaults onto the back of a horse from a take-off ramp.

On the running track

If you're applying to be a runner you'll train on first-class facilities right next to the palaistra – an open air track and a covered one for practice in bad weather, each a *stadion* long (about 200 m). In the Games there is a stadion and a double-stadion race for sprinters. The long distance is 24 stadia. Starting and finishing lines are marked across the sand track by an inset band of stones.

A student being whipped for fouling

Age groups

For lessons and for training pupils are divided according to age. The city's festival of games has similar categories There are events for boys, for 'beardless youths' (late teens) and for adults.

Obey the rules!

◄ Whatever your age you have to put up with strict discipline at all times. The head of the gymnasion (called the *gymnasiarchos*) is a stern person who decides the school's curriculum and appoints the teachers and coaches. His staff punish bad work and fouls with beatings from the long willow canes they all carry.

▼ These older boys are practising for the gymnasion's annual competitions that assess pupils' yearly progress.

Just two stadia to go!

Keeping clean

▲ Since you always exercise naked you won't have to worry about getting the right clothes for the job. The basic equipment for all athletes includes a round flask of olive oil on a cord for hanging it on your peg, a sponge for washing yourself down, and a tool called a *strigil*. You warm up by rubbing yourself all over with the oil; the strigil is used for scraping it off when you've finished for the day. Then you shower in the palaistra washroom, where water trickles into a series of tubs from the lion-headed spouts that line the walls.

▲ A bronze strigil. Its curved blade is hollowed to collect the mixture of oil, sweat and dust you'll be covered in.

In the palaistra

Boxing and wrestling are the palaistra's chief activities. You'll have to be tough to compete, for there aren't many safety rules. In boxing the chief tactic is aiming blows at your opponent's head. There are no rounds and no time limit. You go on until someone drops, and people can get killed. Even so there are boxing competitions for quite young boys.

Wrestling is a test of strength and ruthlessness. There are two forms of the sport. In normal wrestling the object is to throw your opponent to the floor. The second form, the *pancration*, is a really violent type of wrestling that continues on the ground even after a contestant has been thrown.

Anything goes

▶ In pancration wrestling almost anything goes – limb twisting, finger breaking, punching, jumping on your opponent and strangulation. Only biting and the gouging out of eyes are forbidden. Job applicants may like to know that younger boys are not expected to compete in the pancration.

Leather bindings

◀ There are no boxing gloves to cushion the blows. Instead the hands and wrists are bound round with strips of leather up to 4 m long. These help to strengthen the wrists and protect the knuckles.

Hard lessons

◀ A a new type of binding is gaining favour: a piece of fleece-lined leather bound round the forearm, wrists and knuckles. A hard knuckle guard of laminated metal strips gives added protection and increases the harm done to an opponent. The leather bindings are nicknamed 'ants', because they sting an opponent's skin and leave little nicks and grazes behind. The leather used is usually ox-hide. Pigskin strips are banned because they inflict particularly painful wounds that are very slow to heal.

◀ The referee watches with his willow cane ready. Raising one finger signals that you give up.

I give up!

Broken nose

Bruised and battered

▶ This bronze statue of a boxer shows the wear and tear you can expect. He has a broken nose and blood (inlaid in copper) drips from his forehead, nose, cheek and ear.

The pentathlon

Beyond the running track is the practice area for javelin and discus throwing, and for long jump. This is where you train if you want to compete in the pentathlon, which is made up of five events: sprinting, wrestling, jumping, discus-throwing and javelin-throwing. It's a tough contest. Unless you have staying power, don't apply.

The long jump

▼ The long jump is performed to the accompaniment of flute music. Rhythm is crucial to getting the right movement, and the music helps the athlete to establish it. He grasps a weight in each hand and these help to carry him forward.

Discus tips

With his weight on his right foot and ▶ leaning slightly back, the discus thrower steadies the discus at shoulder height. He raises his arm and, as he starts his throw, bends and spins round to propel the discus.

First grip the javelin with your right hand.

▲ Stretching his arms out in front of him, the athlete stands poised for a moment, listening to the flute player to get the right rhythm.

Jumping tips

◀ He does a standing jum without a run up and, as h leaps, swings the weights in front of him. Once in the air they continue t pull him forward. As he descends he stretches h arms and legs forward and, lastly, swings the weights behind for added thrust.

Javelin tips

▼ Javelin throwers wrap a thin leather thong round the javelin shaft, making it end in a loop. This acts as a sling to help propel the javelin forwards. The thong unwinds in flight.

▲ As he runs forward the javelin thrower holds the tip of the javelin with his left hand to press it back against the loop. He releases the tip as he brings his right arm forward, slipping his fingers from the loop as he hurls the javelin. Learning to bind the javelin well is the secret of success.

Discus

Jumping weight

Javelin

Pick

▶ This Ancient Greek vase painting commemorates the pentathlon. It shows a discus thrower and a javelin thrower taking their starting positions. A pair of weights for long jump hangs behind them. The pick is for digging the pit for the jumpers' soft landing.

Competing in the City Games

Each year you'll have a chance, if you are good enough, of competing in the annual Panathenaia, Athens' City Games. Every fourth year the city hosts a much larger festival, the Great Panathenaic Games, open to athletes throughout Greece, with valuable prizes to be won. Events include athletics, horse and chariot racing, and contests for *kithara* playing, flute playing and accompanied singing.

On your marks...

Start line with grooves

◀ This is your starting position, left foot forward, knees slightly bent and arms outstretched. Your toes must be positioned in the two grooves cut in the band of stone that marks the starting line.

Stadion race

▼ The most important event is the stadion race. Its winner will be the hero of the games. If you do well in your training period you could be one of these competitors.

Get set...

▲ Runners take up their positions behind a starting barrier formed of two cords stretched across the track at knee height and at waist height. The cords are stretched between two posts, which are kept in an upright position by the starter. He stands well back, holding a cord which will spring the posts forward when it is released.

Go!

▲ The starter has just cried 'Apite!' (Go!) as he releases the cord that catapults the starting gate to the ground. You're off – good luck!

16

Longer distances

▶ Athletic events are held in the *agora*, the big open market-place. A running track is marked with lanes, each with a post at the far end to show runners in the double-stadion where they must turn. A separate post marks the turning point for long-distance runners.

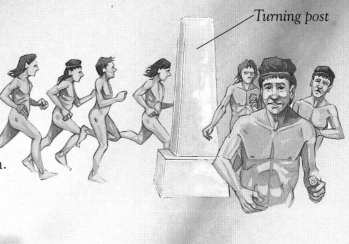

Turning post

Prizes

There are prizes for first, second and third place (and sometimes for fourth and fifth place too). Some are paid in money, some in olive oil in costly jars with an image of Athena on the side. All are valuable. The winner of the boys' stadion gets 50 jars, each holding nearly 40 litres of oil (a total value of around £6,000 in our money).

Athena

▶ Athena, protectress of Athens, watches over the Games. A giant statue of her stands in her temple overlooking the city. You must always remember you are competing in honour of the goddess.

17

At the hippodrome

After your race you can relax and enjoy the other events. The horse races are always exciting. Because they need a long track they are run outside the city on a course known as a *hippodrome*.

Danger!

▼ The four-horse chariot race is run over 12 laps of the hippodrome. There is a turning post but no barrier in the centre of the track. There have been some nasty head-on crashes.

Glory

◄ A winner often has a monument made to celebrate his triumph. This bronze charioteer commemorates a victory in a four-horse chariot race of 474 BC.

FASTER! FASTER!

Stepped starting positions

Starting blocks

▲ The horses start from a V-shaped series of stalls, closed by cords. The cords of the two outer stalls are dropped and their horses take off. They trigger the cord of the next stalls as they pass, and so on until all the horses are running abreast.

Horse trainers

Chariot racing calls for split-second handling of the horses, especially at the turns, and successful teams are famous. Yet it is the owner of the horses who wins, not the charioteer, who is usually a slave or professional driver. In this way a woman can win a prize at the all-male Games if she owns a winning team. Owning and training horses is expensive, so you have to be very rich to compete.

▶ There is also a two-horse chariot race. For both races the chariot is a light vehicle with a metal or wicker cage around the driver's stand.

Keeping fighting fit

Watching the adult events you'll notice that many involve fighting skills. Although the main purpose of the festival is religious, Athens wants all its young men to be able to defend the city and sees the Games as a great boost to military training.

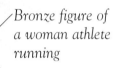
Bronze figure of a woman athlete running

▲ Men and women don't mix publicly in Ancient Athens, so girls take it for granted that they must have separate Games.

War practice

Contests with a military slant include javelin-throwing from horseback to hit a target, and cavalry charges by opposing teams.

Women's athletics

◄ Women have their own four-yearly festival in honour of the goddess Hera, which is held at Olympia like the top all-male Games. Although Athens sends a team, women's sport has a much lower profile here than in Sparta, which prides itself on training all its young people to be tough.

Phyrric dance

◄ These dancers, bearing shields, are from a marble relief celebrating their victory in the pyrrhic dancing contest. This is a sort of military ballet in which competing teams perform movements based on the various skills a fighter needs in attack and defence. The aim is to promote military precision and teamwork.

Torch race

▼ The torch relay race is a high point in the festival. Starting from the famous Akademy gymnasion outside the city, ten teams compete to pass a flaming torch from runner to runner through the streets of Athens to the heights of the Acropolis. The winning team is the first to reach Athena's altar and light the fire for the chief sacrifices of her festival.

Hoplitodromoi

▲ Runners known as *hoplitodromoi* take part in a race in armour, bearing the weight of helmets and heavy shields. Although this race is run over the same length as the double-stadion race, it calls for different skills, requiring special muscle power as well as speed, so it is rare for the same athlete to win both.

At Elis

▼ For the ten months leading up to the games the judges are housed in a special building at Elis, to be given training in the Olympic regulations and the rules of the various events.

Palaistra

Agora

Temple

Judges' lodging

Theatre

Good athletes are ambitious, so you'll certainly be aiming to represent Athens at one of the big inter-state Games. Four cities host these, in a four-year cycle – Isthmia and Nemea twice every four years, and Delphi and Olympia once. If you're chosen for Olympia, the top competition, you'll join other contenders at the little city of Elis, which organises the games. The 50-member Olympic council is based at Elis. Every four years this little city-state is turned into an athletic training town (the equivalent of the modern Olympic village).

Gathering crowds

Athletes bring their coaches and often family and friends as well. Tourists and fans come to watch them, and Elis is soon crowded with people.

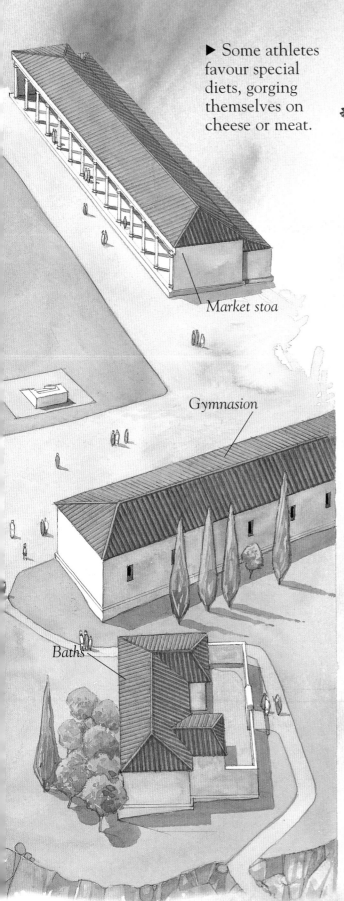

▶ Some athletes favour special diets, gorging themselves on cheese or meat.

Market stoa

Gymnasion

Baths

An athlete arriving at the Games, fit and confident

▲ Competitors must reach Elis a month before the Games start to receive final training from ten judges, newly elected for this Olympic year, who umpire its events. Athletes arriving late are fined, and any who do not pay will be flogged.

Olympic truce

▼ A month before the Games, heralds are sent to every part of Greece to announce the sacred Olympic truce. During this time any war must cease that might prevent safe travel to the games.

Arriving at Olympia

The day before the Games a procession of judges, athletes, trainers, families, friends and onlookers begin the long march to Olympia, where crowds of spectators are waiting to welcome them. Before entering the site the judges must purify themselves. They wash in a sacred spring, and are sprinkled with pig's blood.

Zeus

◄ A giant statue of Zeus, king of the gods, dominates his temple at the heart of the site. It was built by the famous sculptor, Phidias.

▲ The Games are held in honour of Zeus. Every winning athlete adds to that honour through the excellence he has achieved.

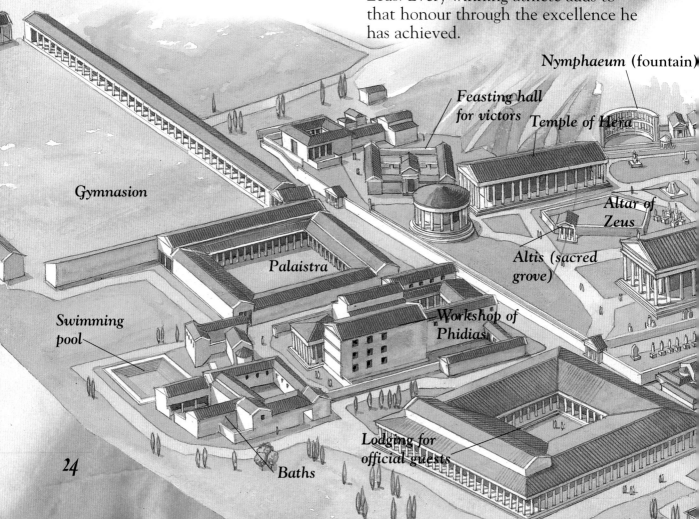

Gymnasion

Palaistra

Swimming pool

Baths

Workshop of Phidias

Lodging for official guests

Feasting hall for victors

Temple of Hera

Nymphaeum (fountain)

Altar of Zeus

Altis (sacred grove)

Registering for the Games

▼ Before the start all athletes attend the *bouleterion* (council chamber), where the judges demand proof of their age and assess how physically close each is to adulthood, in order to assign them to the men's or boys' events. If you're big for your age an upgrade could ruin your chances of winning.

Preparing the running track

▲ Lots of preparation has gone on. Tracks have been dug over, sprinkled with water and rolled smooth. Lanes have been marked with white earth.

◄ In the bouleterion athletes and trainers make a vow, on slices of boar flesh, before the statue of *Zeus Horkios* (Zeus of the oath), that they will do nothing dishonest in the games.

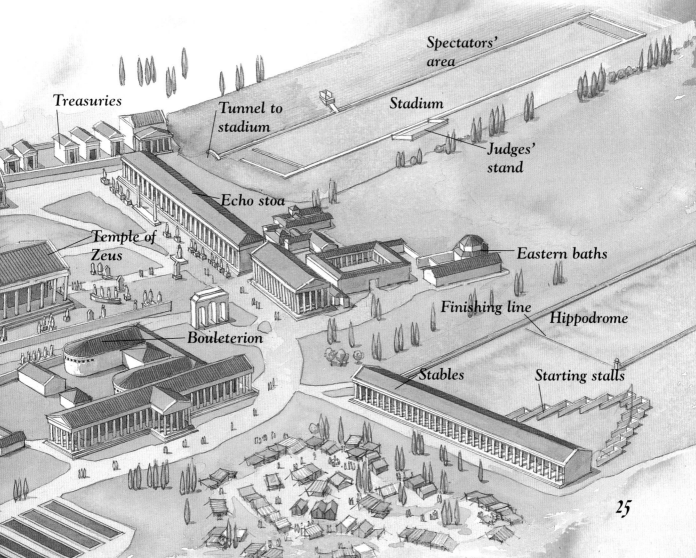

Spectators' area

Treasuries

Tunnel to stadium

Stadium

Judges' stand

Echo stoa

Temple of Zeus

Eastern baths

Finishing line

Hippodrome

Boulerion

Stables

Starting stalls

The Panselinos

The date of the festival is always fixed to ensure that the opening events (horse races and pentathlon) will be followed by a night of the full moon. Since a new day in Ancient Greece was thought to begin at dusk, the full moon (*panselinos*) heralds the religious high point of the Games, the day of the great sacrifice at the Altar of Zeus.

The Altar of Zeus

▼ On the day of the panselinos priests and judges lead a procession to Zeus's altar, a mound formed by the accumulated ashes of past sacrifices.

Sacrifice and feasting

▼ Athletes and ambassadors from the various city-states follow behind with offerings, including a hundred oxen given by the people of Elis.

The oxen are slaughtered at the altar and their thighs burned on the altar-top as an offering to Zeus. The rest of the meat is roasted for the crowd.

▼ Here's something you'll really enjoy. After the great sacrifice the whole crowd joins in a general feasting. Smoke is thick overhead from all the fires on which people are cooking extra delicacies to add to those generous handouts of sacrificial meat.

Roughing it

▶ Spectators have created a tent city around the sacred grove. It's cramped and uncomfortable, especially if it rains, but no one minds. It's noisy too. There are pedlars and fortune tellers shouting; magicians doing tricks; philosophers arguing; poets reciting and applauding each other; and painters and sculptors, hoping for a commission from some winning athlete, setting out their wares.

The Olympic Crown

At Olympia you need to win. There are no prizes for runners-up. Top honours go to the stadion winner; the year's Games are named after him. Ancient Greek historians dated events by saying whose Olympiad they occurred in. So, if you want your name in history, try being a Greek athlete!

Judges' enclosure

▼ The judges watch from a stand near the finishing line. Each winner will be showered with ribbons and flowers by his cheering fans.

The audience awaits

▲ On the last day of events the grassy banks around the stadium are packed with spectators for the footraces. The athletes get ready in a locker room just outside the stadium, and come onto the track through a tunnel under the bank. The runners in each event wait tensely in the tunnel for their race be called.

▼ As each athlete steps from the dark tunnel onto the track, his name and city are announced by a herald. The crowd roars its approval or dislike.

Nikodemos of Athens!

Singing praises

◄ Great Olympic deeds are celebrated in a special kind of poem called a victory ode. Winning athletes, or their admirers, often commission a famous poet to write an ode and to recite it publicly.

A symbolic prize

▼ You don't compete at Olympia for the sake of a fat prize. Every victor has the same reward, a crown of olive leaves cut with a golden sickle from the trees in Olympia's sacred grove. The vase painting below shows a winged figure, representing Victory, giving a winner the most coveted prize in Ancient Greek sport, an Olympic Crown.

Nike, Greek goddess of victory

Wreath of olive leaves

Your interview

An Ancient Greek athlete would know the answer to these questions. Test yourself and see if you're up to the job.

Q1   What do you practise in the palaistra?
A   Swimming
B   Boxing
C   Riding

Q2   What is a strigil used for?
A   Punishing fouls
B   Binding a javelin
C   Scraping the skin

Q3   A friend has been complaining about ants. What has he been doing?
A   Camping at Olympia
B   Boxing
C   Digging the long jump pit

Q4   What is the pancration?
A   A form of wrestling
B   A contest with five sports
C   A city holding inter-state Games

Q5   Which sport uses weights?
A   Long distance running
B   Long jump
C   Chariot racing

Q6   What should you do when someone shouts 'Apite'?
A   Start running
B   Stop running
C   Rush to be first at the food

Q7   What is Elis?
A   A famous female athlete
B   The protective goddess of Athens
C   The meeting place for Olympic athletes

Q8   What does an Olympic winner receive?
A   A golden crown
B   A crown of olive leaves
C   A jar of olive oil

Glossary

agora An open market-place.

Akademy A famous school and gymnasion near the city of Athens.

bouleterion A council chamber.

bronze A brown-coloured metal made by melting together copper and tin.

cavalry Soldiers who fight on horseback.

Citizen In Ancient Greece this meant an inhabitant of a city-state who had the right to decide how it was governed. Tradespeople, women and slaves did not have this right.

colonnade A walkway, open along one side, with columns on the other side, supporting the roof.

curriculum The course of studies taught in a place of learning.

democracy The system of government in Ancient Athens, where every citizen could vote on how the city was run.

discus A large, flat, circular weight, usually made of bronze.

gymnasion A school for boys. The word literally means 'place of naked people'.

herald An official announcer.

infantry Soldiers who fight on foot.

inlaid Decorated, of an object's surface, by having a different material set into it.

kithara A plucked string instrument, a large heavy form of the lyre.

laminated Beaten into a thin metal layer.

Olympiad The four years of an Olympic cycle, from one games to the next.

palaistra An exercise ground.

pancration A violent form of wrestling that did not stop when one opponent was thrown to the floor.

pentathlon An athletic event consisting of five sports.

Sparta The city state that challenged Athens as the major power in ancient Greece.

stadion A measure of length, equal to 600 ancient feet. Also the name of the race of that length (roughly equivalent to the modern 200 m sprint). Plural *stadia*.

stoa A covered colonnade.

strigil A tool for scraping the skin clean.

thong A narrow strip of leather, used like a lace or strap.

wicker A material woven from flexible canes.

Index

Have you got the job?

Count up your correct answers (below right)
and find out if you got the job.

Your score:

8 Congratulations! You deserve the
Olympic Crown.
7 Nearly there. Keep attending the
city games.
5-6 Promising prospects. Try
running with a helmet and shield to
build up your muscles.

3-4 Best stick to the boys' games
for now.
3 or less No chance. Why not try
something less physical. Poetry?

If you think you could live in Ancient Greece, why not take a look at these titles
Spectacular Visual Guides: An Ancient Greek Temple
Battle Zones: Warfare in the Ancient World
or the **Ancient Greek Myths** series:
Theseus and the Minotaur   **The Voyages of Odysseus**
The Twelve Labours of Herakles   **The Wooden Horse of Troy**
The Adventures of Perseus   **Jason the Argonauts**

1 (B) pages 10/11
2 (C) page 9
3 (B) page 11
4 (A) pages 12/13
5 (B) page 14
6 (A) page 16
7 (C) page 22
8 (B) page 29